America

WHITE STAR
PUBLISHERS

Text
Patrizia Raffin

Graphic design
Patrizia Balocco

Contents

2-3 *One of the most spectacular spots in Utah, which in terms of natural wonders is second to no other state in the U.S.A., is Bryce Canyon, a huge abyss which opens up on a fir-covered plateau at an altitude of 8,200 feet.*

4-5 *The New York skyline stands out against the horizon. The panorama of United States metropolises is characterized by skyscrapers, which have become famous for their particular architectural forms.*

6 *A cowboy having a break at sunset beside a giant cactus is one of the most common images of the West: a man, his horse, and nature.*

7 *Like solitary, majestic giants, the high natural reliefs of Monument Valley loom over a desert rendered arid by the burning sun. The Navajo Indians, who once lived on this land, gave these imposing natural towers strange names which were sometimes infantile and rather irreverent.*

8-9 *The Preservation Hall Jazz Band is one of the symbols of New Orleans' musical tradition.*

10-11 *San Francisco at night is lavish with lights and promises thousands of after-midnight entertainment opportunities, as one might expect from such a lively city which is so symbolic of a certain part of the west coast and so free from social prejudice.*

12-13 *Daytona Beach, in Florida, is 24 statute miles long and is frequented by young people who arrive in unusual vehicles. The sandy base is so compact that cars and motorcycles can be parked almost down to the water line.*

14-15 *Oak Alley is the most famous plantation in Louisiana. Built in 1750 by a family of French origin, it is approached along a splendid drive lined by centuries-old oak trees whose trunk circumference is, in some cases, equal to 33 feet.*

© 2003 White Star S.r.l.
Via Candido Sassone 22/24,
13100 Vercelli, Italy
www.whitestar.it

ISBN 88-8095-931-X

Reprints:
1 2 3 4 5 6 7 8   07 06 05 04 03

Printed in Singapore

6

NAL Request
THERS
ITS

WELLS FARGO BANK

Americano
T-SHIRTS
HOT DOGS
FLOATS
BOOGIE BOARDS
RAFTS
CYCLES
FLOATS
HOT DOGS T-SHIRTS
HOT DOGS Coca-Cola T-SHIRTS
FLOATS
SPEED LIMIT 10
SPEED LIMIT 10
SPEED LIMIT 10
TOYOTA

Introduction

There is a pseudo-psychological game which we all play
sooner or later – that of free association of ideas. One
person says a word, "family," for example, and another
replies with the first thing that comes into his head,
giving voice to the image the idea of family creates in his
mind. One can say, "mother," or "house," or
"warmth," or "argument"; it will always be a part of
ourselves that comes to the surface. If 100 individuals of
different ages, social class, sex, cultural background,
family role, and job were to play the the game of free
association starting with the words "United States of
America," we would probably hear 100 different replies,
some of which would be in total opposition to others.
This happens because there is no single archetype to
which we can make reference.

A land of obvious contrasts, a living paradox, or
hell, however one wants to define it, the United States
sums up, coagulates, and reveals the multiple and
contradictory expressions of the planet earth.
Unfortunately, the process of assimilation of so many
different realities is still a long way from being complete.
The United States continuously sends out harsh images
of tentacular metropolises like New York and Los
Angeles, in which the human condition is reduced and
ground into a sort of self destruction, and soft images of
small towns like those in Vermont, in which it is pleasant
to come into contact with other human beings,
following a style of life that is in harmony with the
elementary and cyclical rhythms of nature and
safeguarded by the rules which the community has
established for itself.

Modern-day America presents a many-faceted
reality. It is that freezing, rag-covered bundle sleeping
in the New York subway; it's the beautiful surfer riding
the waves at Big Sur; it's the entire family from a small
town in Nevada spending the weekend at Las Vegas
playing Keno, or enjoying the Magic Kingdom of
Disneyworld. The United States is all-encompassing,
take it or leave it.

Where nature has not thought about creating

differences, with its various combinations of vegetation and climate, fauna and territorial morphology, man has intervened. He lives crushed together in immense urban agglomerates like New York City, with a population of seven million, or reappropriates his individual living space in a state like Utah which has a population density of 15 people per square mile. The population density in North America is, in fact, on average much lower than that in Europe, and America really is the land of open spaces and long roads which cut across the country like arteries, starting from the most vital organs of the system – the cities.

The tourist who decides to visit the U.S.A. and who has no time limit is advised to use the bus or a car and to avoid air travel, which, although it is reasonably cheap and shortens the distances, does not allow the visitor to explore the landscape. In a country which, from East to West, has four different time zones,

16-17 *Cape Cod peninsula, in southern Massachusetts, extends 30 statute miles into the Atlantic and benefits from the warm Gulf Stream. The beauty of Cape Cod's beaches and of the nearby islands of Martha's Vineyard and Nantucket (left and bottom) attract so many visitors in summer that the population doubles. Thus, it is better to visit Nantucket in spring or autumn to fully enjoy the 19th-century atmosphere created by the elegant residences, fishing boats, and typical houses of this village, which, in the last century, was the world's whaling capital.*

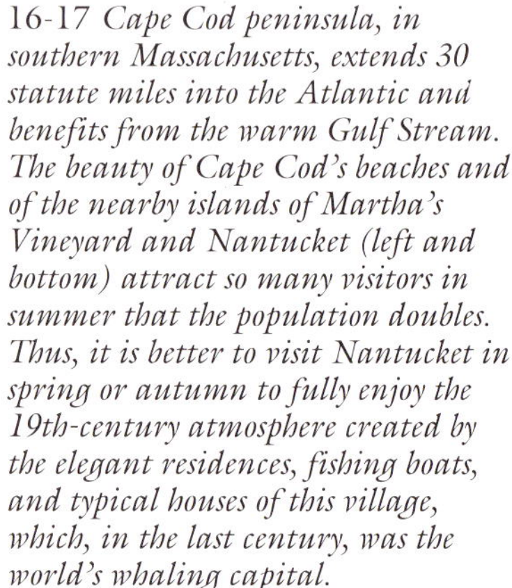

(Eastern, Central, Mountain, and Pacific, each with a difference of an hour from the next), and which extends from the glaciers of Alaska to the Arizona desert and to the warm beaches of Florida (by no mere chance known as the Sunshine State) the visitor who travels by bus or by car has the opportunity of seeing many different varieties of landscape.

The North American landscape has been greatly modified since the arrival of the European colonists a little over two centuries ago. Then, over half of the total surface was covered in forests and now only 32 per cent of the country consists of "green" areas. However, it is still true that the U.S. boasts uncontaminated and extensive wooded areas. In New England there is a mixed vegetation of evergreen conifers and deciduous trees as well as many broadleaf trees, including the magnificent sugar maples of Vermont and New Hampshire, which

Palette while others are more rounded like the dunes which color the horizon with yellow, orange, mother of pearl, and ochre. There are darker brushstrokes where the plants with very deep roots form flashes of color in an arid universe which still palpitates, lives, and forcefully imposes its beauty. Death Valley extends over an area of almost 7,000 square miles in the Mojave Desert. The Indians originally called it Tomesha (Land of Fire) and it was given its current name after the tragic event which happened to a group of gold diggers who succumbed to the infernal heat of the desert on their way to California in 1849. Yet, despite its funereal name, the hidden charm of this valley are to be found on starry nights when the heat lets up and the valley's numerous inhabitants come into the open; among these are goat antelope and wild mules which are the descendants of those famous convoys of 20 mules which brought sodium borate out of the valley at the time of the pioneers. There are also many species of birds including geese, heron, and ducks which visit the small marshes to be found in this vast territory. Human presence in the happy desert, as it has been defined, is very low and there are only 200 residents, the majority of whom are employed in the national park or in one of the two hotels in the region. Human intervention has been limited by the "impossible" climate, with summer temperatures of more than 50° C, but perhaps an intelligent limit has been placed on the use of the territory, and, with due respect to the natural treasures, country roads and structures have been built only where necessary.

America has always felt that its greatest richness was its territory, protagonist of so many western films, that land where palefaced horsemen hid themselves behind the pinnacles of Monument Valley, or rode on mules from one side of the Grand Canyon to the other, traveled up and down the wide prairies of the West, and hunted for bounty to the southwest in the Sonora Desert. Therefore, the United States began to preserve its natural resources from the more evil inhabitants when the concept of ecology had not yet been formulated. Indeed, in 1872, Yellowstone Park became the first national park in the country's history. A park with 200 geysers and 3,000 hot springs, waterfalls, and streams, terraces of travertine stone, swamps and stalactites, thousands of animals including bison, deer, elk, marmots, eagles, and falcons, on display against a backdrop of extremely varied natural beauty almost as if Yellowstone were trying to offer in its 9,000 square miles a sample of all natural marvels. Every year the park is visited by millions of people, and the risk of commercialization is thus very high, but for the moment the characteristics of Yellowstone have been maintained by the people who work in this sector.

Another precaution, albeit a little late, forbids the

collecting of fossils in the Petrified Forest Park, in Arizona. This area of 143,000 sqaure miles contains the largest collection of petrified wood in the world, and here the only color which does not appear is green. The desert landscape may seem inhospitable, consisting as it does of dead trees which have been turned into stone, but it has its own particular beauty and especially in the giant logs the magnificent colors highlight the incredible process of petrification, which began 70 million years ago and which caused the trunks to color themselves as splinters of onyx, agate, and jasper. Once again, it is Arizona which contains perhaps the most famous national park in the U.S.A., the Grand Canyon National Park. Of the 19 canyons which follow the course of the Colorado river from its source in the Rocky Mountains to its mouth in the Gulf of California, these 1,930 square miles contain the most spectacular geological structures, whose projection and shape are due to the erosion of the sedimentary strata which the river created five or six million years ago. The dominant colors are, as one might imagine, ochre and sienna, and the shapes bear witness to the forces of nature which modeled them in a few moments of unheard-of thrusting or by means of a slow progression which has lasted millions of years. Everything speaks of the greatness of nature, and those who do not like technical calculations and scientific explanations can place their trust in the almost mystic emotion which the sight of the Grand Canyon provokes, especially those who observe it from above, from an airplane or a helicopter.

On the border between Arizona and Utah we find that which cannot exactly be defined as an American park, but which quite rightly claims the title of an Indian Park – Monument Valley. In fact, it rises at the heart of the Navajo reserve, and it is the Indians who offer their services as guides for trips into this valley which contains the splendid formations of red sandstone, the peaks of which are more than 984 feet high and which suddenly rise up from the surrounding flat desert and have formed the background to so many Western films. These natural "towers" are equal in form to the buildings of Manhattan, and probably the two opposing images equally attract the interest of the tourist or of those who like to travel at home in the mind and create their own America.

On the other hand, America is in equal measure the frenzied world which throngs in the densely populated quarters of such metropolises as Chicago, Los Angeles, and New York, and that large, spacious country which has space to sell to those who want to travel across it and experience it. The United States is such a composite and complex reality that it would be impossible to try to classify it into well defined categories. There is a working America consisting of world-famous factories

which boast highly advanced production systems, and there is a poor America which lives in squalid ghettos thanks to the handouts of the welfare system or at the mercy of exploiters in the slums. There is the America of West Point with its cadets in their white uniforms and the country of the huge peace marches; there is the America of television "serials" and more conventional "soap operas" and the America which listens to itself in the poetry readings of avant-garde artists. There is the America which lives with the break-up of the family and the America which is attempting to regain higher values through the proliferation of numerous religious sects; the robust and slightly coarse America of the rodeo and other great sporting occasions and the America which burns up its young generations. The United States is a cross-section of varied humanity of opposing mentalities which overlap in a contradictory fashion. America is everything and the opposite of everything, and if we were to play the game of free association starting with the words "United States of America," it would be very difficult to bet on how many would say "Manhattan" and how many would say "Grand Canyon."

A Country Without Frontiers

"America is also and above all open space. Large, boundless, wild stretches portray the innermost sense of the country—the Grand Canyon, a chisel of rocky 'sculptures of breathtaking beauty, and the Rocky Mountains, with their legends of trappers, bears, Indians. And on another lyrical side is Hawaii: a most varied nature, with the palms of Oahu, the beaches and lagoons of Waikiki, the luxuriant vegetation of Maui, the volcanoes, and the warning wrecks of armed ships in the deadly waterways of Pearl Harbor. Forests are to be found throughout the country, as well as plenty of wild beaches with flying birds and sprinklings of foam. Coral reefs run along the islands. And unprofaned glaciers are common in Alaska, turned into the last frontier for oil, the American Siberia."

Guido Gerosa

In 1938 John Ford discovered the incomparable scenario of Monument Valley, and in 1939 this was the setting for his masterpiece *Stagecoach*. It was not only the great success obtained from both critics and public which caused Ford to come back here to film *Fort Apache* in 1948, *She Wore a Yellow Ribbon* in 1949, *The Searchers* in 1956, and *Cheyenne Autumn* in 1964. In his films, the landscape was the absolute co-star alongside the cavalry soldiers and the fleeing Cheyennes. The fact that Ford repeatedly chose Monument Valley is extremely significant and highlights the spectacularity of this natural scenario in which gigantic cathedrals of stone rise up loftily from the tormented ground.

32 top and 33 *The heights of Monument Valley have particular and rather surreal names which were given them by the ancestors of the 30,000 Navajo Indians who still live here and do not want to leave.*

32 bottom *Landscapes sculpted in the rocks cover large areas of the American West. Twisting gorges form the beds of thousand-year-old rivers and bear witness to the remote geological process which produced the wild beauty of the Grand Canyon.*

The Valley of Stone Cathedrals

Landscapes which are literally sculpted into the rock cover the wide spaces of the American West. Twisting gorges, crossed by millenarian rivers' flow, bear witness to the remote geological processes which created the wild beauty of the Grand Canyon. The spirit which animated its creation seems to have remained imprisoned in the monolithic blocks of Monument Valley. Indeed, the most beautiful songs of the Navajo culture speak of the origin of the universe and of that force consisting of rain, wind, and lightning which molded the rocks and **desert**.

The Long Work
of the Centuries

36-37 *Canyonlands National Park extends for more than 250,000 acres in the state of Utah.*

37 top *The San Juan River as it enters Gooseneck State Reserve in Utah.*

37 bottom *An aerial view of Lake Powell and the Glen Canyon National Recreation Area in Utah.*

38-39 *The Grand Canyon, which President Theodore Roosevelt defined as "that superb panorama which every American should see," was formed by the erosion carried out by the Colorado River over the course of 30 million years. In addition, the United States contains many other spectacular landscapes created by the tireless action of nature.*

Another Planet

Death Valley extends over a territory of about 3,000 square miles, 580 of which are below sea level. Death Valley, which the Panamit Indians called "Land of Fire," takes its current name from the tragedy which befell a group of miners from Nevada who lost their lives in this desolate territory in 1849. The natural spectacle offered by this desert has no equal elsewhere in the

world. Sand dunes whose shapes are in continuous evolution alternate with arid valleys in which the sun-dried earth is cracked and split. The heights and the canyons take on a variety of hues, contrasting the blinding light of the sun with the strength of the centuries. The Devil's Golf Course represents the apotheosis of the wild and indomitable beauty of Death Valley: here, a bizarre genius seems to have created delirious sculptures of salt crystals which rise up spectrally from the ground.

42-43 A lunarlike landscape greets the visitor to Death Valley, which was the scenic backdrop to Michelangelo Antonioni's famous film Zabriskie Point.

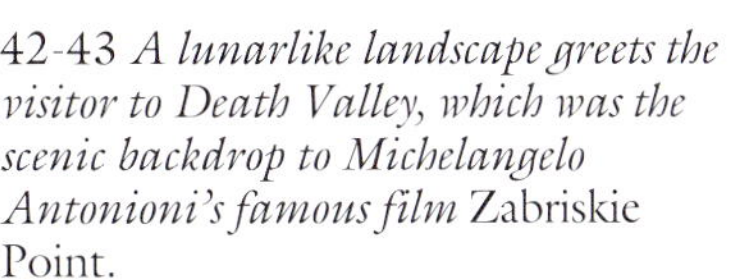

Trees in Prayer

Joshua Tree National Monument in California is a victory of naturalism over capitalism. It was created in 1936 as a protected area, despite pressures from mining companies who wanted to exploit the resources of the area. The name "Joshua Tree" was given by the first Mormon visitors in the 19th century, who saw, in the form of the yucca, a resemblance to Moses' successor, Joshua, at prayer.

Riding the Waves

Big Sur is that stretch of coast to the south of Monterey peninsula and Carmel-by-the-Sea. Monterey was the first capital of California, and among its former inhabitants was Robert Louis Stevenson, who stayed there in 1879 and perhaps drew inspiration for his stories of pirates and hidden treasures. The area is still rather wild, and there are many points at which one's gaze is lost between sky and sea. Carmel-by-the-Sea is a secluded place which has practically become a community of artists who prefer the quiet characteristic streets of this small town, in which neon signs are forbidden, to the bright signs and colorful shop windows of the majority of other towns. On the rocks of Carmel one can often see colonies of seals and sea lions which are accustomed to the presence of man. Here, nature still conserves its charms, and those who love the sea, without wishing the conveniences of the more crowded resorts, can have a pleasant stay. On the other hand, Big Sur is rather crowded and is perhaps the best known stretch of that Californian west coast that is known to all. The landscape, with its cliffs plummeting down to the sea, its highly irregular and indented coastline, and the beautiful ocean, merits the fame it has acquired. Big Sur is a mythical stopping-off point for those who love California and its ocean, but also for those who have fallen under the influence of a certain group of American intellectuals who founded a center here at Big Sur under the aegis of Henry Miller.

A Giant Park

Yosemite National Park extends over 2,980 statute miles of mountains, green valleys, and plain. It contains the largest monoliths in the world, real natural miracles such as Half Dome, El Capitan, North Dome, Sentinel, and Basket. It also includes Upper Fall, a waterfall which is much higher than Niagara, and Mariposa Grove, which contains sequoia trees with a diameter of more than 98 feet.

50-51 *The redwood trees (sequoia sempervirens) in Redwood National Park are the highest in the world, and here we also find the Tall Tree, universally acknowledged as being the tallest tree on earth.*

Uncontaminated Nature

Aspen, Colorado is the most prominent and best equipped downhill skiing resort of the entire West. The notoriously difficult slopes, the powdered snow, and the possibility of staying in the best hotels provide winter sports enthusiasts with everything their hearts could desire. However, despite the fact that it is a busy tourist area, the landscapes of Colorado still maintain a delightful and almost intact nature which also attracts visitors who are not particularly interested in practising sport. In these places one can return to nature, walking along almost deserted roads and fishing on the banks of lakes where there are few people.

Animals in Freedom

The fame of Yellowstone spread across the Atlantic a long time ago. This National Park, set up by President Ulysses S. Grant in 1872, is not only the oldest park in the United States but also the largest in the continental United States, with a surface area of 3,475 square miles. The majority of this territory is in Wyoming, but parts of it also extend into Idaho and Montana. The thing which really makes Yellowstone unique is its geothermal activity, with more than 200 geysers and almost 10,000 hot springs. The park contains the greatest concentration of geysers in the world, exceeding those in other regions such as Iceland, Siberia, and New Zealand. Moreover, it has a remarkable petrified forest in which the trees maintain the upright position which they had had millions of years ago when they were showered with volcanic ash and transformed. Very spectacular and of great interest is also the Grand Canyon of the Yellowstone River: from Artist's Point it is possible to admire the lower falls in all their splendor as they fall into the underlying gorge from a height of 108 feet. However, perhaps the major attraction of Yellowstone is that it provides the opportunity to see thousand of animals circulating freely, including deer, bears, elk, beavers, marmots, and coyote, as well as more than 200 species of birds such as the falcon, the rare whooper swan, and the bald eagle, symbol of the United States of America.

The Spirit of the South in a Great River

The Mississippi rises in Minnesota and curves its way through ten states before emptying into the Gulf of Mexico, where it forms a large delta of 17,760 square miles consisting mainly of marshy terrain, natural canals, and lakes. Despite the passage of time, this great river has maintained its extraordinary charm and its aristocratic elegance, which evoke in the soul all types of fantasies and magical sensations.

The Everglades, an Endless River of Grass

The region of the Everglades extends over an area of 1,300 square miles characterized by grassy stretches, swamps, and a rather hostile nature. In 1947, a national park of 2,300 square miles created. This is constantly patrolled by a well-trained corps of rangers who guarantee protection to a number of animals, including the manatee and the heron, which seem to be threatened with extinction.

Alaska, the Kingdom of Perennial Glaciers

Alaska has been quite rightly defined as the land of records. It is dotted with three million lakes; its "skeleton" consists of tens of thousands of islands and at least 270 glaciers which were formed in ancient times. Its clear skies are crossed by 9,000 aircraft; Alaska has an airplane for every 50 inhabitants and a pilot for every 42. The distances here are enormous, and overland travel is very difficult, especially in the colder season. The territory of Alaska extends over an area of 595,000 square miles, which is twice the size of Texas and equal to a fifth of the entire United States. From 1799 to 1867, this immense land, with its wealth of natural resources, was under Russian dominion before being sold to the Americans for about $7.2 million. In the second half of the last century, during the gold rush, Alaska was taken by storm by adventurers who dreamed of obtaining wealth quickly and easily. Among the pioneers, there was also a young writer destined for fame and glory – Jack London. In his stories he informed the world of the extraordinary uniqueness of these endless glaciers. Alaska is without doubt a strange country, dominated by enormous expanses of unpolluted tundra and taiga, in which caribou and wolves live in a self-regulating equilibrium which requires no human intervention. It was precisely for this reason that two million hectares were transformed into the Denali Nature Reserve, 248 statute miles south of the Arctic Circle, at the foot of the imposing mass of the 20141-feet-high Mt. McKinley.

Cities

"It is the fascination of the great American megalopolises which captures our imagination more than anything else. The influence of cinema and television have made Manhattan and Los Angeles seem more familiar to a young Italian than his home town. We can recognize the spire of the Chrysler skyscraper, or the house Frank Lloyd Wright built for Kaufmann, the Golden Gate and Brooklyn Bridges, and the Guggenheim Museum because they have been impressed on our mind's eye through the images of films, music and the photographs of *Life*."

Guido Gerosa

American cities, unlike European ones, are not linked to a well-defined and centuries-old history. However, their characters are nonetheless evident to the many ethnic groups who have had a part in their development, whether examined from the point of view of the very rich or the very poor.
Most of the cities pulsate with life, and echo to the sounds of the ever-present traffic, mingled with the voices of all the different peoples who have adopted the place as home.

64 top The best view of the city of Seattle is to be had from the top of the rotating restaurant known as the Space Needle.

64 bottom The 4th of July celebrations in Philadelphia have a fundamental importance for every citizen. The celebrations are commensurate with the role this city played in the nation's history. In fact, the Declaration of Independence was signed at Philadelphia in 1776, and for a certain period, the city styled itself with the title of Capital.

65 At 381 metres tall, the Empire State Building is a gigantic modern obelisk made of concrete, steel and stone. It is a monument to a glorious age in New York, the Roaring Twenties

New York, The Big Apple

"It's unique: its neuroses, its fever, its streets, which are dirty but luminous, smelly but perfumed, elegant but tumble-down, are the marvels of the world".

Guido Gerosa

66-67 At sunset Central Park become a relaxing open area. It was designed in 1857 by Frederick Law Olmsted and Calvert Vaux and consists of 840 acres of winding paths and roads, statues, points of interest, hills, ponds and large reservoir. In the background the Triborough Bridge and Queens complete the scenary.

CIRCLE LINE

NEW
YORKER
CUNARD

SONY
SONY
SONY
MIDORI
MELON
LIQUEUR
IMPORTED
MIDORI
melon
liqueur
NOVOTEL
ARTKRAFT STRAUSS
Coca-Cola
COME AND MEET
THOSE DANCING FEET
42ND STREET
W 45 ST
IMPORTED
MOLSON
GOLDEN
Make it Golden
for me and my
friends
FIRE

To speak of this city in terms of figures is perhaps to impoverish it, but it should however be underlined that it has a population of about 7.5 million and that it is visited by 17 million tourists every year, making it the most popular tourist attraction in the western hemisphere. The complexity, variety, and contradictoriness of the Big Apple are excessive even for a New Yorker. In fact there is no archetype of New York, not even in that more or less deformed mirror which is the cinema.

The origins of New York date back to 1626, when the Dutchman Peter Minnewit bought the island of Manhattan from the Indians and founded a colony called New Amsterdam. The name New York was given by the English, who conquered the territory in 1664. Thanks to a particularly favorable geographic position, in the 17th century the city became the obligatory reference point for all those who arrived from Europe. Thus began the expansion of New York along with the birth of a great myth.

Washington, Style and Politics

Three buildings, built in symmetry and inserted into a context of parks and green areas, symbolize the original sense of the city of Washington when the capital had the role of safeguarding civil rights, individual rights, and independence. Overlooking the Potomac River is the Lincoln Memorial, with its 36 columns of white marble, representing the 36 states which formed part of the Union when it was built. Behind this is the obelisk, which reaches a height of 558 feet, and to its rear is Capitol Hill, seat of the Senate and the House of Representatives, symbol of the Federal Union and geometrical center of the city. These splendid buildings are set like gems into an exquisite architectural structure which, with its numerous neo-classical buildings, creates a perfect setting for the legend of Washington. Obviously, a must for any visitor to Washington is a tour of the White House, residence of the Head of State since 1800. George Washington commissioned the French architect Pierre Charles L'Enfant to lay out the city in 1791. A local law has decreed that no building over 13 stories may be built so that the Washington Monument will always be higher than any other building.

Los Angeles, City of Marvels

Incredibly, the first nucleus of Los Angeles was the Saint Gabriel Mission, founded by the Franciscan priests. The discovery of gold first, and then oil, combined to transform this small town into a large city which grows uncontrollably. In 1920 it was already the largest metropolis in the world, and in the 1950s Los Angeles reached the height of its economic expansion. More than any other city it represents the incarnation of success and of that American myth which has been the dream of whole generations. With its luxury villas, Beverly Hills represents the aspirations of millions of people, and Hollywood constitutes the materialization of the wildest dreams of fame and wealth.

74 *The circular towers of the Bonaventure Hotel, designed by architect John Portman, warmly reflect the light of the setting sun.*

75 left *Ultra-modern sculptures and daring constructions characterize the physiognomy of the financial district.*

75 top right *The tourist port for yachts at Marina del Rey is the largest on the Pacific coast and can hold more than 10,000 craft.*

75 bottom right *Los Angeles is a gigantic city, and its road network is more than 11,000 km long.*

76-77 *The city developed without a precise plan, and this led it to expand principally in a horizontal sense. Thus, its panorama is characterized by a vast expanse of low buildings above which rise the skyscrapers of the financial district.*

UNION BANK

San Francisco, Beautiful Place to Live

Resting, like Rome, on seven hills, with the Bay to the east and the Pacific Ocean to the west, San Francisco is blessed with a permanent breeze which does not allow the temperature to exceed 25° C. By choosing an inland suburb, one can also avoid the frequent coastal fog and enjoy the charming climate of San Francisco, venturing up and down the city's steep streets with their famous cable cars, one of

the best known features of the city. However, the true symbol of San Francisco is the Golden Gate Bridge, suspended 656 feet above the waves of the Pacific. Twelve rivers end their course under this bridge, which defies the forces of nature with its 20,000 tons of steel.

80-81 *The Oakland Bay Bridge was opened to traffic in 1936. With a length of about 8 statute miles it links San Francisco and Oakland.*

Chicago,
The City of
Impossible
Challenges

It would be hard to find a city which could be defined as more American because of the frenzy and bustle which pervade Chicago, because of the efforts it makes to outdo itself in launching almost impossible challenges, and for the futurism glorified in its metropolitan architecture. Chicago is truly the city of economic supremacy, skyscrapers, and steel.

Boston, The Cultured City

Boston has been called the most European city in the United States, and when one strolls along Arlington Street where the rich Bostonians built their beautiful mansions and majestic churches, one realizes what is meant by European atmosphere. Here, where the Boston of Henry James maintains its characteristics, there is no exhibitionism nor a false note to disturb the harmonious equilibrium of the city.

New Orleans, City of Joy

The city whose emblem contains an old-fashioned grand piano clearly demonstrates its great love for music. However, this banner also reveals something else about New Orleans. The piano recalls the resistance offered by this confederate city in 1863 against the northern forces under General Sherman. The artillery of the Washington regiment placed this musical instrument in the

center of the fray and, accompanied by its notes, sang old patriotic songs before and after the attacks. The urban layout and the architectural style of the buildings are evident signs of the French and Spanish domination which alternated until 1803, when Napoleon sold the city to the United States of America. The most famous and certainly the most fascinating zone of the city is the Vieux Carr, the French Quarter, on the right bank of the Mississippi, which saw the birth of jazz at the start of the 20th century.

Dallas, The Rich "Big D"

Perhaps it is Dallas which holds the record for stereotypes in the United States. The image which springs to mind is that of the super-rich Texan with a cowboy hat who manages his many petroleum companies from the top of a modern glass skyscraper and who travels by Cadillac to reach his ranch just outside the city. This is partly true, since statistically, Dallas has the greatest number of luxury automobiles in the Western world, and the standard of living is quite high when compared with other cities, which have terrible areas of misery. It should, however, be remembered that oil alone is not sufficient to guarantee wealth and that behind a splendid landscape there is a productive reality based on hard work.

Miami, Millions and Art Deco

The most heterogeneous society in the United States is to be found in Miami. In particular, Cubans and Mexicans form a high percentage of the population, and it has indeed been estimated that half of the entire population speaks Spanish. Geographically, the city is divided by Biscayne Bay into two zones connected by the numerous highways and bridges which cross this stretch of internal sea.

From above, the surface of the water seems to be dotted with artificial islands on which there are luxury villas with private jetties and berths. Along with Miami Beach, Miami benefits from the wealth brought in by the tourist industry which has developed here thanks to the tropical climate and the luxuriant vegetation. Over the years, the city has created infrastructures which have no equal elsewhere in the world, with more than 500 hotels, 400 motels, and more than 4,000 restaurants. Many of these complexes were built by rich Cubans who fled their homeland between 1959 and 1960 with the fall of the Batista regime. In Little Havana, they have partially recreated the charming atmosphere of their country, developing one of the most picturesque corners of the city, pleasantly in contrast with the bright lights and modern architecture of the luxury hotels.

SONG OF AMERICA

Honolulu, Paradise Regained

On the beaches of Waikiki, when King Kamehameha I conquered the territory of Oahu in 1795, the vegetation extended down to the shoreline, and in the surrounding area there were many fields interspersed with inhospitable swamps. Now, years later, the panorama has radically changed, and this beach has become one of the most representative symbols of international tourism.

Some 120,000 people live in an area of no more than 1.1 square miles, in which there are about 450 restaurants and 1,000 shops. The mythical Eden which nestled at the foot of Diamond Head, the extinct volcano which has become the symbol of Hawaii, has been transformed into a modern, rich, and cosmopolitan tourist paradise in which ancient traditions and customs, modified to serve the imperative needs of market and economy, struggle to survive. An eight-lane highway connects the airport to the city, and it is constantly full of traffic. At Honolulu, everything is geared to promoting the tourist industry, which is without a doubt the most important economic activity on the island and the principal source of employment for its inhabitants.

A Style of Life

"Every city and town in America is a world. The people in the United States have a multi-faceted dimension. A boundless planet and a human constellation without end which has undergone a ceaseless process of transformation in the last twenty years and is a source of joy to sociologists, observers of customs, narrators, and film directors.

Raymond Cartier has written that there are fifty Americas, one for every State of the Union. And it's true. The people are like chameleons. At every hour of the day they change skin and color and show themselves in different styles and fashions."

Guido Gerosa

It is not possible to give a single definition to the American style and way of life. One can speak generically of a style of life without presuming to include all aspects of the same. The United States contains an infinite variety of ethnic groups, each characterized by different histories, sentiments, and temperaments. The one thing they all have in common is a deep love for that country which unites and represents them.

96-97 One of the images which most often springs to mind when speaking of the United States and its people is that of the cowboy: those skilful herdsmen who live in direct contact with nature, far from the compromises and the intrigues of business and the chaotic traffic of the large cities.

98-99 There are many different competitions in a rodeo, and they are all spectacular. The cowboys skilfully ride bareback or tame wild horses in a short time. They also wrestle with steers and compete in capturing calves using a lasso.

LABOR DAY
WEEK-END
8
9
10

America at Work

100-101 *Agriculture represents one of the principal sources of income for the American economy and ranges from the cotton fields of Louisiana and the vineyards of California to the endless wheat fields of Iowa.*

102-103 *The crayfish is a fundamental element in the local cuisine of the State of Mississippi, and the crayfish fishing industry flourishes there. In all parts of the U.S.A., fishing is practised and is a relevant source of profit.*

KING ARTHUR

Lazy like a summer in Los Angeles but frenzied like Wall Street, America offers both of its faces to those who wish to get to know it. The fable of Uncle Scrooge McDuck, who created his fortune starting off with a nickel, has been surpassed today. There remains the capitalistic taste for accumulating and increasing economic well-being and the force of a professionalism reached by dint of hard work.

104-105 *Wall Street is America's economic temple. It is here that the fortunes of the country are created and consolidated, and it is here that the strings of the world are pulled.*

A Nation for Sport

Sport is the principal source of amusement, hobby, and pleasure relaxation in the United States. Millions of fans watch and practice a wide range of sports with great passion. Many of them also play, at an amateur level, those same sports which they admire in the large stadiums.

106-107 *The stadiums in which American football is played are often enormous, to cope with the huge crowds who follow this sport. The Superdome in New Orleans is the largest covered stadium in the world with a capacity of 97,000.*

107 left *American football players take to the field wearing light suits of "armor" which are necessary because of the violence of the game.*

107 right *Basketball also has many fans, not only because of the overpowering superiority of American teams in international competitions, but also because children play it in schools from a very early age.*

108-109 *Baseball is the quintessential American sport. Its origin dates back to the initiative of Alexander Cartwright in the last century, but the definitive rules were not laid down until 1859. The picture shows the Los Angeles stadium, in which the Dodgers have excited millions of spectators with their exploits.*

109 top *The oldest hippodrome in the U.S.A., the Saratoga Race Track, has become part of the myth of American society in the same way as Wimbledon is a legend for the United Kingdom. During the racing season, this small city comes to life and becomes the place where the exponents of high society must be seen.*

109 bottom *Golf is a very popular sport in America, and there are many excellent courses with a very high technical level.*

110 *Sailing is the most practised sports in coastal regions. In this picture a sailboat approaches the Golden Gate Bridge at San Francisco.*

110-111 *In the United States all sports are loved and followed in a more or less intense manner, and occasions for creating and watching spectacles are always welcome. This photograph shows a large gathering of hot-air balloonists in Albuquerque, New Mexico.*

The Art of Living

To say that entertainment was born in the United States is certainly excessive, but to claim that the Americans know how to enjoy themselves more than any other people is certainly not an exaggeration. The wide open spaces and the extraordinary natural beauty represent a remarkable starting point, but this would all be worth nothing without the spirit, enthusiasm, and organizational ability of which the inhabitants of the United States constantly give proof. A family holiday in a camper, the magic of Disneyland, an improvised show at Ghirardelli Square in San Francisco, or an important date in Hollywood, everything, really everything in America is a unique occasion not to be missed and to be lived to the fullest.

112 *An American family enjoys the
sunset on a splendid beach in Florida.*

113 *The camper is the vehicle which is
most commonly used to take the family
on holiday, and perhaps, as in this
case, to search for the most charming
corners of Florida.*

114-115 *Daytona Beach, Florida is
thronged with people year round
because of the mildness of the climate.*

Palm Beach owes its birth and development to Henry Flagler, a rich railroad magnate and business partner of the Rockefeller family, who realized the potential of this area as a residential center in 1893 and convinced some of the best known families in the country to move to the south. Within a short time Palm Beach became the preferred residence for members of the high society, and it then developed inexorably. Today North Avenue, with its refined boutiques offering the most exclusive creations of international designers, is considered the most opulent street in the eastern United States.

118-119 If Palm Beach offers a pleasant climate and crystalline water for a serene old age, the natural calm of Georgia proposes a valid alternative for those who wish to enjoy moments of authentic tranquility.

A human jukebox along the streets of San Francisco, a tightrope walker who performs at sunset on the pier at Key West, and students playing music in the main square at Berkley University are all different aspects of a unique way of living and searching for spectacle in daily life. In the United States every spot, square, or crossroad is the ideal place for putting oneself on show, certain that one will manage to attract an attentive and well-disposed audience. America is really the world of spectacle, but at the base of this singular characteristic there is a deep respect for the individual and of his right to express himself even in non-conventional ways, as long as it is not offensive to the dignity of others.

122-123 *Disneyland is in Anaheim, California, 27 miles from Los Angeles on the west coast, and Disneyworld is in Orlando, Florida on the other coast of the United States. Disneyland was created by Walter Elias Disney in 1955, responding to the secret expectations of millions of children and adults. Disneyworld was its continuation 15 years later, enriched quite rightly with a better and more modern concept of an amusement park.*

WALT DISNEY

124-125 *Despite the fact that the epoch in which Hollywood was famous all over the world has long gone, every tourist who visits Los Angeles tries to visit the sidewalk on which the stars have left their handprints and buys a ticket for Mann's Chinese Theater. Here one can relive the atmosphere of the great cinemas of the 1940s, which, with their bas-reliefs, stuccoes, and brocade stage curtains, were temples for the magical rites of showing films that provided the dreamstuff for entire generations.*

The Pioneers of Space

There are three space centers in the United States. The least known is in Alabama, and the more famous ones are the Lyndon B. Johnson Center at Houston, Texas, and the John F. Kennedy Center in Florida, formerly known as Cape Canaveral. Splendid American organization has made it possible for all those curious about space travel to visit the launching pads in all three centers. It is also possible to see perfect reproductions of the Apollo lunar modules as well as to try out mission simulations such as those in which the astronauts train for future missions. This work of promoting space activity has the aim of making the entire nation share in the great progress and the conquests which have been made in this sector, which presents itself as a new frontier, a challenge to the innate pioneering spirit of the Americans.

126 top left *Sophisticated instruments are capable of controlling, from earth, the missions in space.*

126 top right *The shuttle taking off from the launching pad is a spectacle of true technological power.*

126 bottom *Vaguely disturbing technological advances are at the base of progress and space conquest.*

127 *The lunar adventure is now history in the United States. Aeronautical engineering has enabled the achievement of goals which until a few years ago seemed inconceivable.*

128 *American flags outside a bar in Key West, Florida.*